FREDERIC REMINGTON

SOPHIA CRAZE

Crescent Books
A Division of Crown Publishers, Inc.

This 1989 edition published by
Crescent Books, distributed by
Crown Publishers, Inc.
225 Park Avenue South
New York, New York 10003

Produced by
Brompton Books Corp.
15 Sherwood Place
Greenwich, CT 06830
USA

Printed and Bound in Hong Kong

ISBN 0-517-675978

h g f e d c b a

Page 1:
Remington painting *The Indian
Trapper* in 1889.

Page 2:
The Indian Trapper
1889, oil on canvas,
49⅛×34¼in.
*Amon Carter Museum, Fort
Worth, TX*

**Cavalryman's Breakfast on the
Plains**
c.1890, oil on canvas,
22×32¼in.
*Amon Carter Museum, Fort
Worth, TX*

Contents

INTRODUCTION

When we imagine the West as it once was in America – the vast wilderness and the dangers ever lurking, fearsome battles for territory and the rush for gold, cowboys herding cattle on open ranges and countless Indian tribes living in harmony with nature – we are indebted to Frederic Remington, whose artwork still forms and fires the imagination of people around the world.

At the age of 19, Frederic Remington was a robust, sandy-haired youth when he first arrived in the heart of the Wild West in the sumer of 1881 – the moment he had been waiting for since childhood. From his home state of New York he had "gone west" in search of his dream. One night in Montana, as Remington sat by the campfire with an old-timer who had gone west much earlier, he realized that his dream was fast disappearing. Reminiscing about this meeting twenty-five years later he wrote:

> The old man had closed my very entrancing book at the first chapter. I knew the railroad was coming. I saw men already swarming into the land. I knew the derby hat, the smoking chimneys, the cord-binder, and the thirty-day note were upon us in a restless surge. I knew the wild riders and the vacant land were about to vanish forever – and the more I considered the subject the bigger the forever loomed . . . Without knowing exactly how to do it, I began to try to record some facts around me, and the more I looked the more the panorama unfolded.

Remington's youthful passions for horses, tales of the military, and the great outdoors led him, and so many of his day, to seek fortune and adventure in the West. It soon became apparent that he would not make his fortune in business, ranch-ing, or prospecting; his gold lay in his passion for drawing, painting, and sculpting enduring images of the restless spirit of the West.

Remington recreated the world of thrills and romance of which all young boys dreamed. As he said, "I paint for boys, boys ten to seventy." It was the narrative elements of his paintings that brought them so vividly to life. Although he is best known for his art work, which was usually finalized in his studio in the East from sketches he made out West, he also wrote numerous articles and books about his adventures. Through Remington's work easterners had the opportunity to experience vicariously the excitement of the Wild West.

Frederic Sackrider Remington was born on October 4, 1861, in Canton in upper New York State. At this time wagon trains carrying settlers had been rolling west for several decades; the railroad, which for many heralded the beginning of the end of the Wild West, was also steaming steadily westward. Between half a million and a million American Indians, who had formerly been free to live throughout North America, had been bribed, battled, and coerced into moving further and further west into smaller and smaller territories. Nonetheless, the sundry tales of western lore that were recounted around the dinner tables of many eastern homes were fodder for Frederic's fertile imagination.

The Civil War had erupted six months before Frederic was born. When Frederic was only two months old his father, Seth Pierre Remington, left his family and flourishing newspaper business to join the war. As a lieutenant colonel of a regiment that he had helped to establish, Seth served four long years in the U.S. cavalry. Seth's stories of his military exploits im-

Opposite: A wagon train of settlers migrating west along the Oregon Trail, passing the landmark known as Devil's Gate in Wyoming.

Right: *Held Up* (1867), Newbold Trotter. Moving east-west, transcontinental railroads often crossed the north-south migration of bison herds.

Below right: As a teenager Frederic sketched this watercolor of his father, Seth Pierre Remington, a lieutenant colonel during the Civil War.

Below: A watercolor sketch of Custer's Last Stand, one of many western scenes by Frederic while at Highland Military Academy.

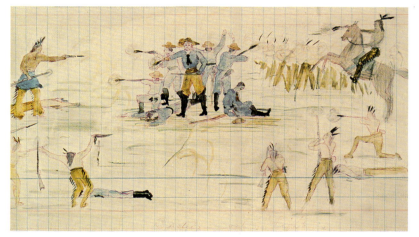

pressed his young son, further enhancing Frederic's longing for high adventure.

Frederic was a boy's boy, who explored the outdoors with a passion. In the idyllic rural setting where he grew up, he preferred to spend his time boxing, hunting, fishing, climbing trees, hiking, swimming, or caring for the horses at the local fire station, rather than studying for school. When confined to his desk he would daydream, drawing sketches of horses, soldiers, cowboys and Indians in the margin of his notebooks. His venturous diversions and his lack of interest in academics concerned his mother, Clara Remington. From her perspective it was important that Frederic be well educated in order to achieve the type of status and success as befitted the son of a prominent eastern family.

In an effort, perhaps, to foster a sense of discipline and responsibility in the rowdy young teenager, his parents sent him to Highland Military Academy in Worcester, Massachusetts, in the fall of 1876, the same year that Lt. Colonel George Custer fought his famous "Last Stand." Despite Frederic's strongly nurtured idealism of military life, he rebelled against its rigid regulations. But he made a niche for himself at Highland, as he became known for his spontaneous sketches of the life that so many of his peers also craved – the excitement of war and of the raw frontier.

Excerpts from Frederic's letters to another boy named Scott, who shared his passion for drawing, reveal Frederic's perseverance in refining his drawing, as well as his penchant for particular subject matter: "You draw splendidly, and I admire your mode of shading, which I cannot get the 'hang' of. Your favor-

ite subject is soldiers. So is mine." But later on he told Scott: "Don't send me any more women or any more dudes. Send me Indians, cowboys, villains, or toughs, these are what I want."

Not until Remington enrolled at Yale as an art student in the fall of 1878 did he receive any formal instruction. During college Remington came to admire the work of two European painters, Jean Baptiste Edouard Detaille and Alphonse Marie de Neuville, who were noted for their meticulous renditions of the Franco-Prussian War. The young apprentice was inspired by their masterful technique, but also awed by it and seriously questioned whether he could ever reach such heights.

The American artists of the time who were highly regarded for their western scenes had also received their training in Europe and were superb technicians. These included painters such as Albert Bierstadt, Karl Bodmer and Alfred Jacob Miller. But for Remington their paintings lacked the vitality of action and adventure of the West that was so vivid in his own mind. Although he was not aware of it then, he could have found a kindred spirit in his contemporary, Charles Russell, who was destined to follow a similar course. Russell, known as the "cowboy artist," was entirely self-taught, and his style was even less formal than that of Remington.

Remington's experience at Yale had only a few high points. His drawing teacher, John Niemeyer, was considered by many to be unsurpassed in his field. But given that the academic approach to art largely consisted of drawing from plaster casts of classical sculpture, Remington was bored. He found freedom from the classroom on the football field as a rusher for Yale's 1879 team. His football captain was Walter Camp, today known as "the father of American football."

Remington made some progress in art and also made a life-long friend in the only other student in his art class, Poultney Bigelow. It was Bigelow who turned the *Yale Courant* into an illustrated college weekly, the first in America. Remington was one of the paper's art contributors; his first piece was one of a series of cartoons in the November 1879 issue titled "College Riff-Raff."

All in all, however, Remington felt constricted and discon-

tented at Yale. When his father died in February 1880, Remington was bequeathed a modest inheritance which allowed him to feel somewhat independent. Not long before he would have graduated, he left Yale, much to his mother's chagrin. He dreamed of the West but, succumbing to familial and societal pressure, he found one job and then another as a clerk. Inevitably, Remington's restless spirit railed against this sedentary occupation.

Fortunately for Remington, an unexpected meeting at county fair in Canton, New York, set off a series of events that would lead him toward his destiny. He was introduced to a young woman named Eva Adele Caten who was visiting a

mutual friend. He fell furiously in love with this vivacious, fair-haired beauty and soon rushed off to Gloversville, New York, to request her hand in marriage. But her father rejected the proposal because of Remington's financial instability. Dejected, Remington determined to go west to seek his fortune so that he could return as he put it, "a millionaire," and prove himself worthy to claim Eva for his bride.

Remington's first trip was relatively short. He immersed himself in the culture of the West with an impatient passion. An able horseman, he soon learned how to throw a lariat. He mastered the six-gun and never shied away from a fight. He explored more land west of the Mississippi than many who lived there, always attracted to those places and people least affected by Manifest Destiny, the westward flow of "civilization." He traveled through the Dakotas, Wyoming, Kansas, Montana, the Oregon Trail, the Santa Fe Trail and treacherous territories pioneered by such legendary figures as Kit Carson and Jedediah Smith. He sought out the truly western experience wherever he went, spending time around the encampments of various Indian tribes, riding with cowboys on wagon trains and on horseback through the open cattle range, and following the Indian war trail. He found the company of rugged individuals – trappers, prospectors, mountain men, and outlaws. After only two and a half months he returned east with a portfolio bulging with sketches.

He enjoyed seeing his first drawing in print when *Harper's Weekly* published a redrawn version of his "Cowboys of Arizona" on February 25, 1882. While this initial success gave Remington some confidence, he remained unconvinced he could make a living with his art. When he turned 21 in the fall of 1882 and received the bulk of his inheritance, he headed west again and bought a sheep ranch in Peabody, Kansas. Here,

too, he befriended every western character he could find. He was locally known for his late-night drinking revelries with cowboys and old-timers in saloons. He also socialized with more notable members of society such as the local sheriff and John Mulvaney, painter of a well-known version of Custer's Last Stand. But as success at ranching was not forthcoming and the lure of adventure pulled him, in the spring of 1884 he sold his ranch and wandered even further into the Southwest.

Upon his return to Kansas City, Remington sold some sketches that he had made on his travels. But the fortune that he had set out to acquire so that he could marry Eva still eluded him. He invested what was left of his inheritance into a saloon;

subsequently, his partners swindled him. In spite of his destitute state, he went back east and somehow managed to convince Eva's father to allow them to marry. The young couple returned to Kansas City and set up house.

This period of domesticity did not last long due to their poverty and the cruder living conditions of the Wild West. Although Remington continued to submit sketches for publication, he met with little success. Eva found it difficult to adjust to this tenuous life. Thus they thought it best for Eva to return east to wait for her husband, while he continued to seek his fortune through his art, which he finally acknowledged as his true vocation. Remington set off once more into the far Southwest with nothing much more than his horse and saddle. It was make or break.

He tried his hand at prospecting in Arizona. There, the battle for supremacy was all around him. The U.S. cavalry was in hot pursuit of Geronimo, the Apache leader who was thought to be hiding in the area. As Remington and his fellow prospectors sat around the campfire one night discussing Geronimo, they suddenly saw three Apaches sitting across from them. Ready to assume that one of their visitors was Geronimo, Remington and his friends reached for their guns only to discover that the Indians were simply hungry. The tension of the moment was not lost on Remington who, writing about the incident later for *Century Magazine*, revealed how events such as this could stir his imagination:

> I mused over the occurrence. For a while it brought no more serious consequences than the loss of some odd pounds of bacon and flour, yet there was a warning in the way those Apaches could usurp the prerogatives of ghosts.

From Arizona, Remington ventured north into Indian territory where he spent time with the Comanches. He particularly admired this tribe's skill in handling and breeding horses. By this time Remington had amassed a huge portfolio of work, and in the summer of 1885 he returned to Eva in the East. After this trip Remington, bowing to Eva's wishes, never lived in the West again. But later he would return periodically to wander and sketch on his own or on assignment.

The Remingtons experienced another lean season, this time in Brooklyn where they lived with friends. They had moved to New York to be nearer the major publishing houses. Although most editors recognized Remington's raw talent, they thought his illustrations lacked the necessary polish for publication. In addition, Remington's subject matter was not in keeping with the prevailing concerns of the nation amid the Industrial Revolution. In order to secure investments for its burgeoning railroads, factories, foundries, mines and banks, America as a young debtor nation was anxious to create a favorable impression with Europe – which precluded promoting the idea that the West was still untamed.

Fortunately, by the new year of 1886, Remington's persistence won out. The art editor of *Harper's Weekly*, Henry Mills Alden, who had already published two of Remington's sketches that were redrawn, put his illustration "The Apache War –

Indian Scouts on Geronimo's Trail" on the cover of the January 9, 1886 issue. Although it is acknowledged that, as the art historian Brian Dippie has commented, "the picture exhibits all the faults of Remington's early work," this endorsement of Remington's work by America's most popular weekly was pivotal in his career. In the meantime, Remington's ultimate goal was to achieve recognition as a serious painter. Acknowledging his need for technical training, in March he enrolled in the Art Students League.

In the same year Remington illustrated a story by Frances C. Baylor for *St. Nicholas* and renewed his acquaintance with his former classmate, Bigelow, who was then editor of *Outing* magazine. When he showed Bigelow his work, Bigelow was so taken by the drawings that he did not even recognize Remington until he noticed the signature. Entranced that fate had brought them together again, and by the genius that he saw in Remington's rough sketches, Bigelow bought the entire portfolio. After Remington's first illustration appeared in *Outing* in December 1886, Bigelow, as he attested, "loaded him with orders likely to keep him in every number of the magazine for two or three years."

Remington was now on his way to achieving the recognition

Opposite: One of Remington's earliest published illustrations, "The Apaches Are Coming," in *Harper's Weekly*, January 30, 1886.

Opposite below: Another Remington woodcut, "Signalling the Main Command," appeared in *Harper's Weekly*, July 17, 1886.

Right: A rare glimpse of Geronimo (on horseback) with his Chiracahua Apaches in Arizona Territory.

Left: Pen-and-ink drawing, "Broncho Busters Saddling," first appeared in *Century* magazine in February 1888 and later was included in Theodore Roosevelt's book, *Ranch Life and the Hunting Trail*.

Below: "A Fight in the Street," one of 64 Remington illustrations reproduced in *Century* in 1888.

that he pursued so tenaciously. However, by June of 1886 his impatience with formal instruction and his urge to further explore the Southwest compelled him to join army expeditions in Arizona, again tracking warring Apaches. At this point, he had spent only three months studying at the Art Students League. Thereafter, he relied solely on his exacting eye and determination to improve his technique. Once back in his studio in New York, he reworked the many sketches he had made on these western expeditions.

At this time, suddenly Remington received more illustration work than he could handle. His painting was also attracting attention. In 1888 his painting *Return of a Blackfoot War Party* won two prizes in the annual exhibition of the prestigious National Academy of Design in New York. He had several other paintings exhibited that year in addition to 54 illustrations reproduced in *Harper's Weekly*, 32 in *Outing*, 27 in *Youth's Companion*, and 64 in *Century*. His illustrations for *Century* were published for a series of articles by another Old West enthusiast, Theodore Roosevelt. These drawings appeared later that year in Roosevelt's book, *Ranch Life and the Hunting Trail*, which contained a total of 99 Remington illustrations.

By the late 1880's Remington's success was assured. His work

struck a chord with the American people and was propelled into the forefront of public consciousness. In the midst of a depression, Americans were looking back to better times and realized that the Wild West, symbol of the American pioneering spirit, had all but disappeared. Remington's illustrations and paintings – along with the writings of two other easterners, Owen Wister and Theodore Roosevelt – became extremely

Left: Remington on the prairie in Wyoming.

Below: "Buffalo Hunter at Full Gallop Loading His Gun with His Mouth," in *The Oregon Trail* (1900) by Francis Parkman.

Opposite top: From a series by Eadward Muybridge. Sequential photography disproved nineteenth-century theories of animal locomotion.

Opposite: Remington sculpting *The Buffalo Horse*, surrounded by his treasured souvenirs of the West in his New Rochelle studio.

Opposite right: *The Wounded Bunkie* (1896), Remington's second sculpture.

Opposite below: Jim Gabriel and a band of Sioux, members of the popular Buffalo Bill's Wild West Show, c.1904.

popular, echoing as they did the public nostalgia and growing sense of guilt over the destruction of the Wild West and the Indian way of life.

The Remingtons' new-found prosperity enabled them to afford an apartment of their own, one near Central Park in New York. There, Remington arranged a makeshift studio in the parlor, filled it with souvenirs of his western adventures, and set to work with characteristic vigor. Despite his wild and woolly reputation, he regularly maintained a disciplined schedule. He got up at six o'clock every morning and worked until mid-afternoon. Then, to appease his restless spirit, he would take a long walk or go for a ride on horseback through Central Park. In the evening he would return to the studio to plan the improvements and revisions for the following day. Remington continued to enjoy the recreation of sharing a bottle between friends at night, often talking until dawn. Although he disdained much of New York's social life and was not impressed by its celebrities, he built long-lasting friendships with such men of renown as Theodore Roosevelt, Rudyard Kipling, Owen Wister and Augustus Thomas.

In 1890 Remington received an important assignment – to illustrate Henry Wadsworth Longfellow's popular poem, *The Song of Hiawawtha*, with 22 full-page color plates and nearly 400 drawings. Two years later he illustrated Francis Parkman's classic, *The Oregon Trail*. Parkman wrote in the preface that Remington's "pictures are as full of truth as of spirit, for they are the work of one who knew the prairies and the mountains before irresistible commonplace had subdued them."

In 1890 unrest was brewing out West again. Thirty-thousand Sioux, under the leadership of Sitting Bull, congregated in the

Bad Lands of South Dakota. Remington jumped at the opportunity to experience some action and joined a scouting party in search of Sitting Bull. He returned to New York two days before the massacre of the Sioux befell at Wounded Knee on December 29, 1890. Although he had missed the battle, he accumulated ample material to write and illustrate a number of articles on the famous Sioux uprising.

Remington was in his heyday – success back East, action out

West. In 1892 he finally had a stable for his horses and a spacious studio in a comfortable home in New Rochelle, New York. Remington often used the wealth of western artifacts that bedecked his studio as props for his models. Resigned to living in the East, he surrounded himself with as much of the West as he could gather in his travels.

Remington was not known for his open-mindedness. Coupled with his enthusiasm for the West was his disdain for Europe and all things European. In the summer of 1892 when his old friend Bigelow took Remington on a trip to North Africa, Russia and England, the provincial Remington was not impressed by much. The high point of his visit to London was watching Buffalo Bill's Wild West Show. In addition, Remington's overtly masculine style made him uncomfortable with women other than Eva. The West that he knew and portrayed included no women, but only horses and the typically rugged males with whom he could relate.

Remington's love for horses never waned. He often said that he wanted the epitaph, "He knew the horse." Remington was, in fact, the first artist to create true-to-life pictures of horses in action. Initially as an illustrator, he referred to photographs of his own and of others to check his details. Many critics suggest that Remington based his pictures of horses in motion on the photographs of Eadweard Muybridge, whose stop-action photography was published in the 1880's around the time when Remington began to work as an illustrator. Remington departed radically from the conventional artistic style of the day and depicted galloping horses with all four feet off the ground; although some doubted the accuracy of Remington's vision, it was confirmed by Muybridge's photographs.

The year 1895 was an important turning point for Remington. His writing talent was given due recognition with the publication of his book *Pony Tracks*. Moreover, Remington moved into the medium of clay with sculpture.

That summer the noted sculptor Frederic Ruckstull advised Remington in how to begin a sculpture from one of Remington's drawings of a bronco buster. It was a project that would have daunted many experienced sculptors – to model from clay a bucking bronco on his hind legs with a rider on its back – but Remington plunged enthusiasticaly into this medium. "I have always had a feeling for mud," he remarked casually. That fall in garnering acclaim with his first bronze, *Bronco Buster*, Remington fulfilled his ambition of elevating his reputation as an illustrator to that of fine artist. Over the years he sculpted 23 pieces, nearly all of them equestrian compositions.

However, there was still one ambition that Remington had

Above left: Teddy Roosevelt's Rough Riders were the last elite U.S. cavalry regiment.

Above: Remington at his island retreat, Ingleneuk.

Left: "Twilight of the Indian" (1867) expresses Remington's nostalgia for the Old West.

Opposite above: Shoshone farm lands near Cody, WY, c.1904.

Opposite below: From a series in *Century, Cosmopolitan* and *Collier's*, 1889-1909.

not realized – to experience first-hand a large-scale modern war. In February 1898 when war broke out in Cuba, he headed off as fast as he could to illustrate the action. Although Remington, like many others, was disenchanted with the reality of the Spanish-American War, he produced a series of articles and illustrations for *Harper's Weekly* and Hearst's *Journal*, in addition to some memorable canvases. One of his best known paintings from that time, *Charge of the Rough Riders at San Juan Hill* also served a political purpose, in depicting Theodore Roosevelt leading the charge. Roosevelt was being groomed for the New York gubernatorial campaign, and Remington's picture contributed to the legend of Roosevelt as a soldier. It was unusual for Remington to feature any public figures; he liked to paint the ordinary man, and this was apparently the only instance when Remington used his art to sway public opinion. In fact, Remington made a point of not instilling a message in his art, but simply represented the facts as he saw them.

Remington made his break from illustrator to painter when *Collier's Weekly* commissioned him to paint an exclusive series of pictures to be reproduced in full-color, double-page spreads. The theme and subject matter was left entirely up to Remington, thereby freeing him to paint without constraint. Although he earned less money illustrating by painting then by drawing, he retained the original canvasses, which began to sell for high prices. Some of his most famous paintings were produced for *Collier's;* for example, *His First Lesson* appeared in *Collier's* on September 26, 1903, followed by other such masterpieces of his later years as *Fight for the Water Hole, The Stampede* and *With the Eye of the Mind.*

The success that met his paintings in *Collier's* was reinforced by the many exhibitions of his original paintings held in the early twentieth century. Everyone agreed, as the foremost art critic of the day, art editor of the *New York Herald Tribune*, wrote that, "the mark of the illustrator disappeared and that of the painter took its place." Remington responded in kind,

A Dash for the Timber
1889, oil on canvas, 48¼×84⅛ in.
Amon Carter Museum, Fort Worth, TX

Pages 22-23:
Cavalry in an Arizona Sandstorm
c.1889, oil on canvas, 22⅛×35¼ in.
Amon Carter Museum, Fort Worth, TX

Pages 24-25:
Aiding a Comrade
c.1890, oil on canvas, 34×48 in.
The Hogg Brothers Collection,
Museum of Fine Arts, Houston, TX

Dismounted: The Fourth
Troopers Moving the Led Horses
1890, oil on canvas,
34 1/16 × 48 15/16 in.
Sterling and Francine Clark Art
Institute, Williamstown, MA

Through the Smoke Sprang the Daring Soldier
1897, oil on canvas, 27⅛×40 in.
Amon Carter Museum, Fort Worth, TX

Pages 30-31:
Battle of War Bonnet Creek
c.1897, oil on canvas, 27×40½ in.
The Thomas Gilcrease Institute of American History and Art, Tulsa, OK

The Fight for the Waterhole
1901, oil on canvas, 27×40 in.
The Hogg Brothers Collection,
Museum of Fine Arts, Houston, TX

Rounded-Up
1901, oil on canvas, 25×48 in.
Sid Richardson Collection of Western Art, Fort Worth, TX

A Reconnaissance
1902, oil on canvas, 27×40⅛ in.
Amon Carter Museum, Fort Worth, TX

Pony Tracks in the Buffalo Trails
1904, oil on canvas, 30¼×51¼ in.
Amon Carter Museum, Fort Worth, TX

The Last March
1906, oil on canvas, 30×22 in.
*Frederic Remington Art Museum,
Ogdensburg, NY*

Fired On
1907, oil on canvas, 27⅛×40 in.
Gift of Walter T. Evans, National Museum of American Art,
Smithsonian Institution, Washington, D.C.

The Sentinel
1907, oil on canvas, 36×27 in.
Frederic Remington Art Museum, Ogdensburg, NY

On the Southern Plains
1907, oil on canvas, 30⅛×51⅛ in.
The Metropolitan Museum of Art, New York, NY
Copyright © 1982

COWBOYS AND OTHER FRONTIERSMEN

Remington's attraction to drawing cowboys stemmed as much from his admiration for the horses they rode as to the wild life they led. The cowboys Remington encountered were rugged characters who herded cattle on the long drive from Texas to the northern ranges, traveling across unclaimed and often uncharted territory on their broncos. During the solitary months on the trail, they struggled against the perils of droughts, storms, and turbulent rivers, always alert to the threat of a stampede or attack from unfriendly Indians.

Remington had studied the history and the lineage of horse breeds and arrived at the conclusion that

As a saddle animal simply, the bronco has no superior . . . He graces the Western landscape, not because he reminds us of the equine ideal, but because he comes of the soil, and has borne the heat and the burden and the vicissitudes of all that pale of romance which will cling about the Western frontier.

The western writers of the day romanticized this image of the cowboy, and Remington set the scene. From his early intricately detailed drawings to his later more impressionistic and most lauded works, he featured the reckless cowboy and his bronco – ranching, herding, and hunting. For Remington and many of his contemporaries, the cowboy epitomized what a man should be – tough, courageous, occasionally warm, and capable of enduring great hardships.

The original cowboys were the Mexican vaqueros on the Rio Grande. From the vaqueros the Texan cowboys adapted much of their equipment – the big-horned saddle, the spade bit, rawhide rope, and their expressions such as *remuda* (spare horse) and lariat. By the time Remington lived in the West the Texan cowboys had assumed their own unique style, which Remington documented for posterity.

Remington also recorded the lives of other adventurers – the settlers, pioneers, prospectors, mountain men, trappers and outlaws who were an integral part of the western scene. As he traversed the wildest parts of the West, Remington searched for the old-timers whose experiences he would assimilate to broaden his perspective and his art. In his later years he painted the wilderness of New York State where he spent more and more time canoeing, fishing, and enjoying the sunsets at his island home Ingleneuk.

Poultney Bigelow, the editor of *Outing* magazine who early on recognized Remington's genius, complemented Remington upon seeing his drawings:

Here was the real thing, the unspoiled native genius dealing with Mexican ponies, cowboys, cactus, lariats and sombreros. No stage heroes these; no careful pomaded hair and neatly tied cravats; these were the men of the real rodeo, parched in alkali dust, blinking out from barely opened eyes under the furious rays of the Arizona sun.

The Cowboy
1902, oil on canvas, 40¼×27⅜ in.
Amon Carter Museum, Fort Worth, TX

The Sentinel, 1889
1889, oil on canvas, 34×49 in.
Sid Richardson Collection of Western Art, Fort Worth, TX

Turn Him Loose, Bill
1892, oil on canvas, 25×33 in.
The Anschutz Collection, Denver, CO

The Puncher
1895, oil on canvas, 17¾×14⅞ in.
Sid Richardson Collection of Western Art, Fort Worth, TX

What an Unbranded Cow Has Cost
1895, oil on canvas, 28⅙×35⅛ in.
Gift of Thomas M. Evans, Yale University Art Gallery, New Haven, CT

The Fall of the Cowboy
1895, oil on canvas, 25×35⅛ in.
Amon Carter Museum, Fort Worth, TX

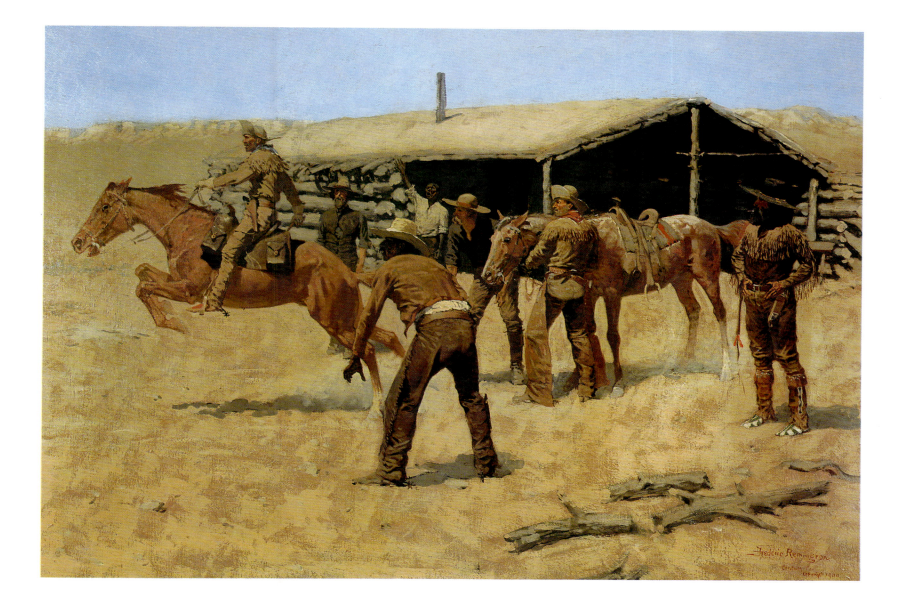

Coming and Going of the Pony Express
1900, oil on canvas, 26×39 in.
The Thomas Gilcrease Institute of American History and Art, Tulsa, OK

The Old Stagecoach of the Plains
1901, oil on canvas, 40¼×27¼ in.
Amon Carter Museum, Fort Worth, TX

His First Lesson
1903, oil on canvas, 27¼×40 in.
Amon Carter Museum, Fort Worth, TX

The Emigrants
1904, oil on canvas, 30×45 in.
The Hogg Brothers Collection, Museum of Fine Arts, Houston, TX

A Taint in the Wind
1906, oil on canvas,
27⅛×40 in.
Sid Richardson Collection of
Western Art, Fort Worth, TX

Howl of the Weather
1906, oil on canvas, 40×27 in.
Frederic Remington Art Museum, Ogdensburg, NY

Guard of the Whiskey Trader
1906, oil on canvas, 30¾×21⅛ in.
Gift of Mr. and Mrs. Samuel L. Kingan,
University of Arizona Museum of Art, Tucson, AR

An Old Time Plains Fight
1904, oil on canvas, 27×40 in.
Frederic Remington Art Museum, Ogdensburg, NY

The Stampede
1908, oil on canvas, 27×40 in.
The Thomas Gilcrease Institute of American History and Art, Tulsa, OK

Return of the Blackfoot War Party
1887, oil on canvas, 28×50 in.
The Anschutz Collection, Denver, CO

The Buffalo Hunt
1890, oil on canvas,
34×49 in.
*Buffalo Bill Historical Center,
Cody, WY*

Captured
1899, oil on canvas,
27×40⅛ in.
Sid Richardson Collection of
Western Art, Fort Worth, TX

The Snow Trail
1908, oil on canvas, 27×40 in.
Frederic Remington Art Museum, Ogdensburg, NY

Pages 86-87:
The Grass Fire
1908, oil on canvas, 27⅛×40⅛ in.
Amon Carter Museum, Fort Worth, TX

FREDERIC REMINGTON

With the Eye of the Mind
1908, oil on canvas, 27×40 in.
The Thomas Gilcrease Institute of American History and Art, Tulsa, OK

Indian Warfare
1908, oil on canvas, 29½×50 in.
The Thomas Gilcrease Institute of American History and Art, Tulsa, OK

Indians Simulating Buffalo
1908, oil on canvas, 26¹⁵⁄₁₆×40⅛ in.
Gift of Florence Scott Libbey,
The Toledo Museum of Art, Toledo, OH

The Buffalo Runners, Big Horn Basin
1909, oil on canvas, 30⅛ × 51⅝ in.
Sid Richardson Collection of Western Art, Fort Worth, TX

Apache Medicine Song
1908, oil on canvas, 27⅛×29⅞ in.
Sid Richardson Collection of Western Art, Fort Worth, TX

Pages 94-95:
The Smoke Signal
1909, oil on canvas, 30½×48½ in.
Amon Carter Museum, Fort Worth, TX

The Scalp
1898, bronze, 25⅞ in. high
Amon Carter Museum, Fort Worth, TX

The Wicked Pony
1898, bronze, 22 in. high
Amon Carter Museum, Fort Worth, TX

The Norther
1900, bronze, 22 in. high
The Thomas Gilcrease Institute of American History and Art, Tulsa, OK

Coming Through the Rye
n.d., bronze, 27½ in. high
Buffalo Bill Historical Center, Cody, WY

The Cheyenne
1902, bronze, 20⅛ in. high
Buffalo Bill Historical Center, Cody, WY

The Mountain Man
1903, bronze, 28 in. high
Buffalo Bill Historical Center, Cody, WY

Polo
1904, bronze, 22 in. high
Frederic Remington Art Museum, Ogdensburg, NY

The Old Dragoons of 1850
1905, bronze, 24×46×19 in.
Frederic Remington Art Museum, Ogdensburg, NY

The Rattlesnake
n.d., bronze, 22 in. high
Buffalo Bill Historical Center, Cody, WY

The Buffalo Horse
1907, bronze, 25⅞ in. high
The Thomas Gilcrease Institute of American History and Art, Tulsa, OK

The Savage
1908, bronze, 11¼ in. high
Frederic Remington Art Museum, Ogdensburg, NY

The Stampede
1910, bronze, 23×48×20 in.
Frederic Remington Art Museum, Ogdensburg, NY

LIST OF COLOR PLATES

Picture Credits

All pictures were provided by the credited museum or gallery except those supplied by the following:
Amon Carter Museum, Fort Worth, TX: 13(middle right)
The Bettmann Archive: 11(bottom)
Brown University Library, Anne S.K. Brown Military Collection: 10(below)
Frederic Remington Art Museum, Ogdensburg, NY: 1, 8(above right), 9(below), 10(above), 11(middle), 12(above and below), 13(middle left), 14(above right)
Kansas City Public Library, Missouri Valley Special Collection: 9(above)
Kingston-upon-Thames Museum and Art Gallery, Eadweard Muybridge Collection: 13(top)
The Library of Congress: 14(above left), 15(below)
National Archives: 6, 11(top), 15(above)
The New York Public Library: 8(below)
The R. W. Norton Art Gallery, Shreveport, LA: 7(below left and right), 14(below)
The C. M. Russell Museum, Great Falls, MT: 13(bottom)
Smithsonian Institution: 7(top)
Yale University: 8(above left)

Acknowledgments

The publisher would like to thank Janet Wu York, who edited and did the picture research for this book; and Mike Rose, who designed it.